GET ACTIVE!

GYMNASTICS

Alix Wood

WAYLAND
www.waylandbooks.co.uk

All sports can be dangerous. Do not attempt any of the skills in this book without supervision from a trained adult expert.

Wayland
First Published in Great Britain in 2019 by Wayland.
Copyright © Hodder & Stoughton

Published by permission of Gareth Stevens Publishing, New York, NY, USA.

Produced for Wayland by Alix Wood
Art direction and content research: Kevin Wood
Editor: Eloise Macgregor
Editor for Gareth Stevens: Kerri O'Donnell
Consultant: Mike Beagley, Falcons Gymnastics, Barnstaple, UK

HB ISBN: 978 1 5263 1166 5
PB ISBN: 978 1 5263 1167 2

Photo credits:
Cover, 1, 21 top, 24, 27 top and middle left © Shutterstock;
4 © Dmitry Berkut/Shutterstock; 22 top © muratart/Shutterstock;
all other photos © Chris Robbins.

Acknowledgments
With grateful thanks to gymnasts Adam Tobin, Sophie Jeffery, Byron Day-Rogers, Daniel Mock, Ibrahim Kany, Joe Cemlyn-Jones, Phailin Ferracin and Ryan Owen.

Printed and bound in China

Wayland
An imprint of
Hachette Children's Group
Part of Hodder & Stoughton
Carmelite House
50 Victoria Embankment
London EC4Y 0DZ

An Hachette UK Comany
www.hachette.co.uk
www.hachettechildrens.co.uk

MIX
Paper from responsible sources
FSC® C104740
FSC
www.fsc.org

CONTENTS

WHY DO GYMNASTICS?

Gymnastics is fun and keeps you fit. Doing gymnastics can help your self confidence and make you strong and flexible.

There are so many ways you can enjoy gymnastics. There are five main types of gymnastics: artistic, **rhythmic**, trampolining, acrobatic and **synchronised**. Artistic gymnastics is the one most people see on TV. It is divided into men's and women's. Men have six events: the vault, pommel horse, parallel bars, high bar, rings and floor. The women have four events, vault, bars, beam and floor.

Rhythmic gymnasts do dancelike routines with a ribbon, rope, hoop, club or ball. Sometimes groups of rhythmic gymnasts do routines together.

Trampolining and tumbling involves moves on a trampoline, a mini-tramp or tumbling on a special bouncy floor. Acrobatic gymnastics is a competitive partner sport where two or more gymnasts perform routines. Synchronised gymnastics involves a team of gymnasts typically either all men or all women.

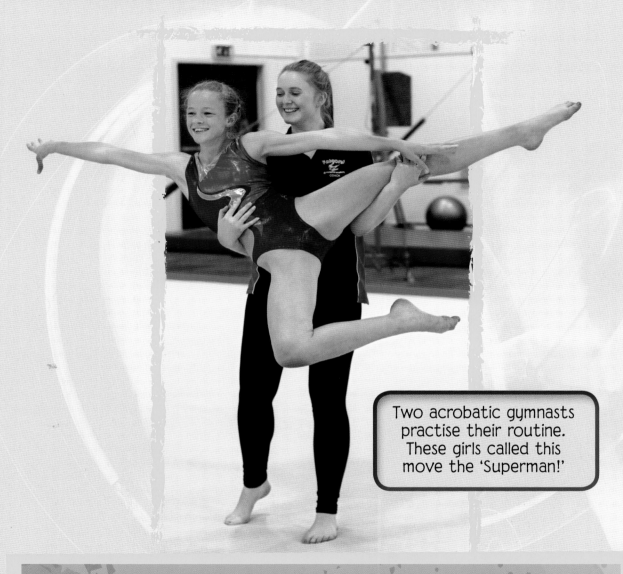

Two acrobatic gymnasts practise their routine. These girls called this move the 'Superman!'

TRY THIS

Most people who reach the top level of gymnastics start when they are very young. Don't let that put you off, though. You can start at any age. Contact a club near your home and see what classes they have that interest you.

WARMING UP

Doing gymnastics can cause injuries. It is vital to do a good warm-up. A warm-up stretches your muscles and helps you to avoid injury.

A good warm-up should start with some **cardio** exercise, such as a five minute jog. Then you should warm up all the different parts of the body. Do arm circles to the front and back to warm up your shoulders. Gently stretch out your wrists and ankles and turn your neck. Roll your ankles around to flex the joint. Make sure you stretch your **hamstrings** and **calves** well before you attempt an exercise such as the splits. Do the same gentle exercises to cool down after a gym session, too.

A gentle jog is one of the best warm-ups.

To stretch your hamstrings, arms and calf muscles, try these exercises. With stretches it is important not to strain yourself. Stretch gently as far as you can without feeling any pain.

This hamstring stretch helps warm up your leg muscles. Squat down with your hands flat on the floor.

Lift up your back, keeping your hands on the floor. Don't worry if you can't get as straight as this boy.

Gently try this centre split. Sit and straddle your legs as wide as is comfortable. Keep your legs straight and toes pointed. Lean forward keeping your back straight. Hold the stretch.

7

FLOOR WORK

In gymnastics, the floor refers to a specially prepared exercise surface. In competitions, an event performed on the floor is called a floor exercise.

The men's floor routine consists of tumbling. It must contain both forwards, sidewards and backwards tumbling as well as a single leg or arm balance. The women's floor routine is performed to music and has gymnastic, acrobatic and dance elements. In your routine you must show off your best moves in a very short space of time.

It may take many months of practice to learn to do a full split like this one. Take it gradually.

TRY THIS

After a good warm-up and plenty of stretches, you could try to do the splits. Stand in a straddle position and gradually slide down as far as you can. Keep your back knee tucked in, not facing out to the side. Try staying in that position for around 30 seconds. Remember to cool down after the exercise, too.

Once you have practised the splits on the floor, you can use it in your floor routine in other ways. In gymnastics clubs the floor is used to practise for moves to be done on other apparatus also.

When you become good at gymnastics, these are the kind of floor moves you can do!

The spring floor has springs or rubber foam and plywood, which makes the floor bouncy. It softens the impact of landings and lets the gymnast gain height when tumbling.

Simple Floor Gymnastics

Here are a some floor work moves to try. If you get good, you could try them on the beam!

A headstand may seem simple, but it is important to get it to look strong, elegant, **symmetrical** and steady. Make sure you practise on a cushioned floor, with someone to help hold your legs in case you wobble.

Kneel down. Place your head on the floor. You will balance on the front of your hairline.

Raise your bottom and walk your feet towards your hands. Raise your feet from the floor. Hold in a tuck position with your knees bent.

Straighten your legs. Keep them together, with your toes pointed towards the ceiling.

A bridge is another floor exercise that can be used in routines. It is useful as a warm-up exercise for your spine, too.

Lie flat on your back.

Bend your knees. Place your hands palm down by your ears. Your fingers should be pointing at your shoulders.

Take a deep breath. Push up with your arms and legs and arch your back. Bend your knees and lower yourself gently back down.

TRY THIS

At first do a bridge on the balls of your feet. It's easier.

11

THE POMMEL

The pommel is a piece of equipment used by male gymnasts in competitions.

It takes a great deal of strength, **coordination** and skill to perform moves on the pommel. There are some cool ways that gymnastics coaches teach students the skills. One of them involves a bucket! Putting the gymnast's feet in a bucket on a rope allows the gymnast to contentrate on learning the correct body position.

Using a bucket on a rope helps to teach gymnasts how to do a circle.

The equipment the gymnast in this picture is using is called a mushroom. It is closer to the ground and has a larger surface to move around than the pommel, so it is good for beginners. Coaches will often draw a clock face in chalk on the floor and teach the student to change positions at the different numbers.

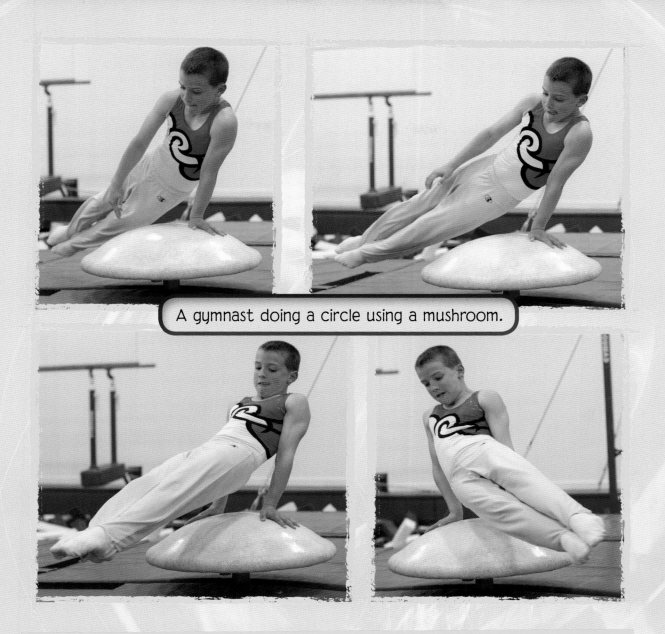

A gymnast doing a circle using a mushroom.

TRY THIS

Build up your arm muscles by practising push-ups. Push-ups can be done anywhere there is a flat surface. Get on the floor and support yourself by your toes and arms. Place your hands under your shoulders. Keep your body straight and lower yourself until your chest nearly touches the floor. Breathe out as you push back to the start position.

Useful Exercises

While doing a pommel horse routine, the whole weight of your body is supported by your wrists.

Gymnasts will often wear wrist supports when they are working on the pommel. In a move such as the circle, below, your hands are constantly lifting up and down and changing position as you swing around the pommel. You also use your **core** muscles in your **torso** to keep your body straight. Your shoulder muscles are important, too.

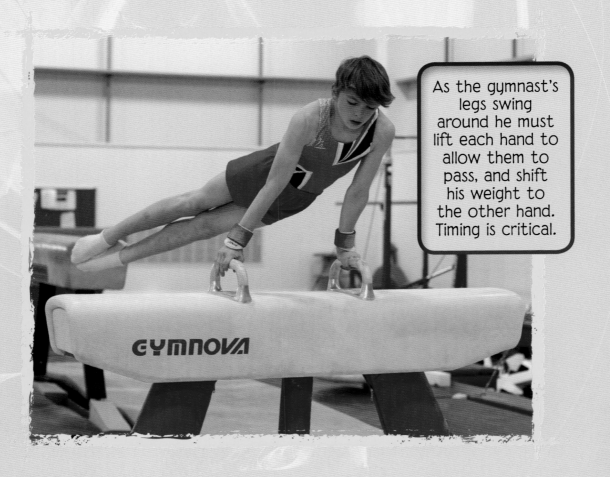

As the gymnast's legs swing around he must lift each hand to allow them to pass, and shift his weight to the other hand. Timing is critical.

The best training for the pommel is by repeatedly doing lots of pommel exercises! At home you won't be able to practise using a pommel horse or mushroom, however. You can still do exercises to help you. Try this L-sit lift.

L-sit lifts are great for gymnastics core conditioning. Sit on the floor with your legs straight out in front. Make sure the area behind you is clear in case you fall backwards. Place your hands on the floor, just in front of your hips. Your hands can be flat or on knuckles. They can also be forwards, sidewards or backwards. Press yourself up into an L-sit and hold it for a few seconds.

Once you have mastered the L-sit you could try a V-hold. Try to lift your legs as high as possible. Keep your elbows straight.

TRY THIS

In the background of the picture on the left a gymnast is doing a manna. These are very difficult to do! Notice he has his hands facing in the other direction. Keep practising your L-sits and V-holds and you may build up to trying a manna.

USING THE BARS

There are three types of bar used in gymnastics. The high bar and **parallel** bars are used by male gymnasts. The uneven or **asymmetric** bars are used by female gymnasts.

The uneven bars

Some gymnasts wear hand guards to help them grip the bars. There are several different ways of holding the bars. Pictured below is an overhand grip. If you turn one hand the other way around it is called a mixed grip. Both hands the other way around is called a reverse or underhand grip.

Hand guards give support and help gymnasts train for longer.

Gymnasts put chalk on their hands and on the apparatus.

Gymnasts chalk their hands to help remove perspiration and reduce slipping.

The high bar is one of the most exciting gymnastics events. Gymnasts perform giant swings and spectacular **dismounts** that can include multiple flips or twists. The bar is over 2.75 m off the ground. A controlled dismount from this height is very difficult to do. You can practise a controlled dismount by jumping off something low onto a mat.

Land with both feet at the same time. Bend your knees and sit back. Use your arms to steady yourself. Try not to take an extra step if you can.

When you feel you are steady, raise your arms and smile!

Parallel Bars

A competition parallel bars routine usually includes a swing above the bars, below the bars, and a skill that involves releasing and regrasping both bars.

The gymnast mounts the apparatus either from a springboard or the floor. The gymnast must do every move with precision. Routines are judged on skill difficulty and **execution**. Points are deducted for bent knees, flexed feet, spread legs and hops on the dismount landing. Points are added for skill difficulty. A gymnast who makes a mistake during a routine of more challenging skills might score higher than a gymnast who performs a less challenging routine flawlessly.

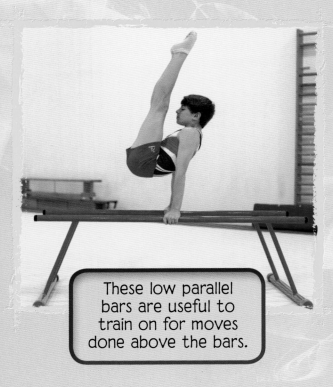

These low parallel bars are useful to train on for moves done above the bars.

TRY THIS

A lot of local parks have a set of parallel bars. See if one near where you live has a set. Always practise with someone else. You can help each other get on and off safely.

Practising a handstand on the floor will help build up your skill and get your muscles ready for the parallel bars. Practise against a wall at first and use mats.

Kick one leg up, then follow with the other leg. Keep your arms and legs straight, and your legs together. Point your toes towards the ceiling. Don't arch your back or bend at the hips. Push down through your palms so your shoulders and arms are fully extended, and your elbows are locked out.

Lift your arms up over your head. Lunge forwards and place both hands in front of you on the floor, shoulder-width apart, 30 cm away from the wall. Keep your fingers spread out and facing forwards.

A handstand on the parallel bars

VAULTING

A competition vault is all over in a few seconds. Packing all the gymnast's skill into that short space of time is the challenge. You have to get every part right.

A gymnast must run fast, and explode off the springboard to get as much height and **rotation** as possible. When gymnasts first learn the vault they often slow their run when they approach the board. Practise helps them stop slowing down.

A good run up and strong jump from the board means the gymnast can fly through the air!

Practising sprinting is a great way to improve your vaulting skills. Warm up by jogging for a few minutes and doing some stretches. Then sprint fast for a short distance. Make L shapes with your arms and swing your arms forwards and backwards. This helps your speed. You can even just stand and do the arm movements at home. Your muscles will build up if you repeat the movements until you feel the burn.

A vault run up area is 25 m long. You can choose how long your run up is. At the end of the run the gymnast jumps onto the springboard.

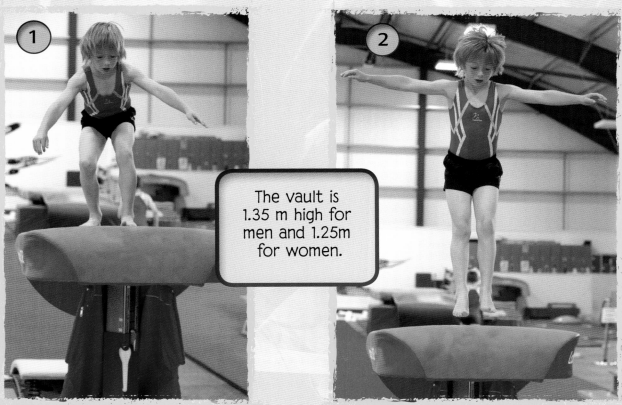

The vault is 1.35 m high for men and 1.25m for women.

When you are starting out, try jumping onto the vault.

Then jump off. Remember to bend your knees when you land to absorb the fall.

THE BEAM

When you are performing on a 10 cm narrow beam, there is no room for mistakes.

Gymnasts practise on the floor and a low beam first. Once they can do a move well there, they move up to the high beam. Even something simple takes practice before you can perfect the skill on the beam. Gymnasts will have a spotter to help them. A spotter is a person, often your gymnastics coach, who stands ready to catch you if you fall.

Try this straddle L-sit. Sit in a straddle, with your legs straight and apart. Lean forwards with your shoulders over your hands. Try to lift your heels off the ground.

Once you have perfected the move on the floor, try it on a low beam and then a high beam.

Try perfecting this cartwheel on the floor, first.

Start your cartwheel with your arm that is on the same side as your front foot. Place your other arm a shoulder length further down the line.

Imagine a straight line on the ground. With both feet along the line, look at the point ahead where you will place your hands.

TRY THIS

- The order goes: one arm down, opposite leg up, other arm down, opposite leg up.

While upside-down, look at your hands. This will help your balance. Land one foot, then the other. Straighten up.

RINGS

Gymnasts perform moves from two rings which hang from a rigid metal frame. Only men compete in rings at a competitive level.

> The gymnast must use their strength to keep tension on the rings.

> This L-sit is a static strength hold. It takes strength to keep still and stop the straps from wobbling.

Gymnasts need to have very strong arm muscles before they are allowed to use the rings. A good swing on the rings is harder than on the high bar. Gymnasts do swing, strength and hold elements in their rings exercises. They usually include a swing to held handstand, a static strength hold and an aerial dismount. In competitions, gymnasts are penalised for having bent arms in strength elements or using the straps to support or balance themselves. There are also deductions if the cables swing a lot during a routine.

1

2

The rings are a long way up. Your coach may have to help you to grab hold of them.

You may need to use handgrips on the rings. Make sure you have mats underneath you.

3

4

You can try to pull yourself up into an L-sit. Have a spotter help you.

When you get good, you can try to lift your hips over your head. Your spotter should help hold you.

TRAMPOLINE

Trampolining develops air sense, spatial awareness and strength. It is a competitive Olympic sport. Gymnasts perform routines while bouncing on a trampoline.

There are some important safety measures to understand before you begin to trampoline. Trampolining should always be supervised. Never trampoline alone. It is very easy to hurt yourself. It is a good idea to wear socks. This stops your toes from entering any gaps in the trampoline webbing.

A trampoline move in a tucked position

TRY THIS

In competitions, moves are usually performed in one of the following three basic shapes:

tucked	With knees clasped to chest by hands
piked	With hands touching close to feet and both arms and legs straight
straddle	Legs creating a triangle with hands on ankles

Competitive trampolining routines consist of combinations of 10 contacts with the trampoline bed. You need to learn to land in these four positions – feet, seat, front and back. A routine must always start and finish on your feet.

To do a pike, jump up with your hands raised above your head. Keep your legs together and straight.

Bring your arms down and forward and touch your feet. Hold your stomach in. Slide your hands back along your legs and to the side of your body until you land on your feet.

A safe foam area surrounds this gym's trampoline

ACROBATIC

Acrobatic gymnastics, or acro, is a partner sport. Each pair or group competes in three routines to test their balance, power and skills.

This move is most definitely not for beginners! The stand on shoulders is a great acro move. It must only be learned with correct instruction, at a gym, and with spotters and safety mats. Do not try this at home.

The girls join hands in a cross grip. Girl A is on the left. Girl B is on the right.

Girl B semi-squats. Girl A places her right foot on Girl B's thigh. They join both hands.

③

When Girl A is steady, Girl B shifts her grip to Girl A's calves. Girl A extends her arms.

⑤

Girl A steps up, using downwards arm pressure to help lift herself. She turns around and places her left foot on Girl B's shoulder.

Only practise this move with an instructor and with a spotter who can catch you if you start to fall.

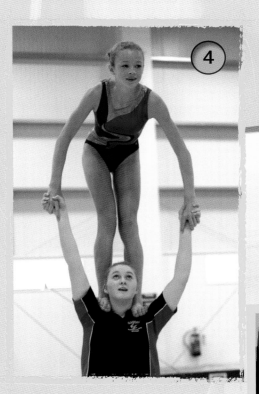

④

Holding both hands to steady herself, Girl A stands up.

TRY THIS

Join a gymnastics club to see if you like it. It's a great way to challenge yourself.

GLOSSARY

asymmetric Not identical on both sides of a central line; lacking symmetry

calves The back portion of the lower leg

cardio Concerning the heart

coordination Smooth working together, such as good muscular coordination

core The deep muscles in the torso

dismounts The action of getting down from something

execution Carrying through something to its finish

flexible Capable of being bent

hamstrings A group of muscles in the back portion of the upper leg

parallel Lying or moving in the same direction but always the same distance apart

rhythmic Of, relating to, or having rhythm

rotation The act of rotating especially on an axis

spatial awareness The ability to be aware of oneself in space

symmetrical Having, involving, or showing symmetry, that is a close agreement in size, shape, and relative position

synchronised Cause to occur or operate at the same time or rate

torso The trunk of the human body

FOR MORE INFORMATION

Books

Heneghan, Judith, *Mad About: Gymnastics* (Wayland, 2016)

Mason, Paul, *Sports Skills: Gymnastics* (Franklin Watts, 2017)

Websites

BBC Get Inspired: How to get into Gymnastics
www.bbc.co.uk/sport/get-inspired/28689820
Gives information and advice about getting into gymnastics.

Gymnastics Technique and Training
www.drillsandskills.com
A forum for gymnasts, coaches or anyone who just wants to learn about gymnastics skills.

Teens Health
kidshealth.org/teen/safety/sports_safety/safety_gymnastics.html
Gives advice about gymnastics safety.

INDEX